Looking at Plants

Roots, stems and leaves

Sally Morgan

Belitha Press

First published in the UK in 2002 by
Belitha Press
A member of **Chrysalis** Books plc
64 Brewery Road, London N7 9NT

Editor: Jean Coppendale
Designer: John Jamieson
Artwork: Chris Forsey
Picture researcher: Sally Morgan
Educational consultant: Katie Kitching

ISBN 1 84138 435 6

British Library Cataloguing in
Publication Data for this book is
available from the
British Library.

Printed in Hong Kong
10 9 8 7 6 5 4 3 2 1

Picture acknowledgements:
E = Ecoscene, P = Papilio, CI = Chrysalis
Images

Front Cover (main), 3 & 12 E/Andrew Brown;
Title page, 24 & Cover (insets) P/Robert
Pickett; 2 & 8 (T) E/Frank Blackburn; 4 & 5
(T) E/Frank Blackburn; 5 (B) E/Richard Glover;
6 CI/Robert Pickett; 6-7 E/Sally Morgan; 7
E/Ian Harwood; 8 (B), 30 (T) & Cover (insets)
E/Frank Blackburn; 9 E/Joel Creed; 10 & Cover
(insets), 10-11 E/Sally Morgan; 11 (main) & 32
P/Ken Wilson, (inset) P/Robert Pickett; 13 (T)
E/Andrew Brown, (B) E/Whitty; 14 P/Robert
Gill; 15 (T) P/Neil Miller, (B) P/Frank Young; 16
& Cover (insets) E/Wayne Lawler; 17 (T),
(inset) CI/Robert Pickett, (B) P/Mike Buxton; 18
E/Sally Morgan; 19 (T) E/Gryniewicz, (B)
E/Andrew Brown; 20 E/Sally Morgan; 21 (T)
E/Wayne Lawler, (B) E/Sally Morgan;
22 E/Anthony Cooper; 23 (T)
CI/Robert Pickett, (B) & 31
E/Andrew Brown; 25
(T) E/Andrew Brown,
(B) CI; 26, 27 (T) & 30
(B) E/Sea Spring
Photos, 27 (B)
P/Robert Pickett.

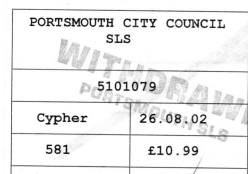

Contents

Words in **bold** are explained in the glossary on page 30.

Introduction

Plants trap sunlight which they use to make food. The food is used by the plant to grow roots, stems and leaves. The parts of the plant above the ground are called the **shoot.** Out of the shoot grow the stems and leaves. The roots are found below ground. These hold or anchor the plant in the ground and take up water.

*The leaves and flower of the snowdrop grow from a **bulb**. Roots grow and spread out under the bulb and hold it in place in the ground.*

4

There are many different types
of plants and their leaves, stems
and roots vary in shape and size.

The leaves make all the
food that the plant needs.

The leaves of this fan palm
are held out to trap as much
light as possible. Without
light, the plant cannot
make food.

Leaves for food

Most leaves are green. This is because they contain a green substance called **chlorophyll** (klor-o-fill).

Plants need chlorophyll to make their food. They use a gas called **carbon dioxide** from the air and water from the ground. When sunlight shines on a leaf, the carbon dioxide and water join together to make sugar and **oxygen**.

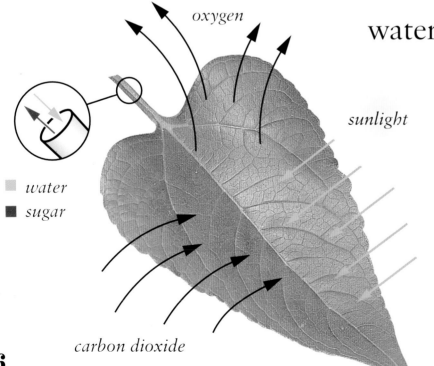

oxygen

sunlight

water

sugar

carbon dioxide

Plants make food during the day when sunlight shines on their leaves.

If you look up through the branches of a tree you will see that the leaves grow so that each leaf gets as much light as possible.

Oxygen is a gas found in air. Some of the oxygen is used by the plant, but the

*Not all leaves are green. A **variegated** leaf has green areas and white or yellow areas. Food is only made in the green areas of the leaf.*

rest moves out of the leaves into the air.

Animals use the oxygen to breathe.

Leaf shapes

petiole   mid rib   vein

*The beech leaf has a simple oval shape with a **petiole**. The petiole is a short length of stem that joins the leaf to the main stem.*

Leaves are thin and flat. They are supported by **veins** that criss-cross the leaf. The veins carry water to all parts of the leaf. The central vein that runs up the middle of the leaf is larger than all the others. This is called the **mid rib.**

The horse chestnut leaf is made up of five or more leaflets of different lengths. They are joined together at their base.

8

Leaves have many different shapes. Some leaves are oval in shape. Others are heart-shaped and some are the shape of a hand. The edge of the leaf may be jagged or **spiky**.

Some leaves are made up of many smaller leaves called leaflets. These are called **compound leaves**.

Water lilies have rounded leaves that lie on the surface of the water. The leaves are strong and can support the weight of small animals such as birds and frogs.

Leaf protection

Many animals like to eat leaves. The plant has to protect its leaves from these animals. Some have tough or spiky leaves that are difficult to eat.

The leaves of this acacia tree are protected by large spines. The spines stop animals such as giraffes from eating all of its leaves.

The holly has prickles or spines along the edge which stop animals from eating the leaf.

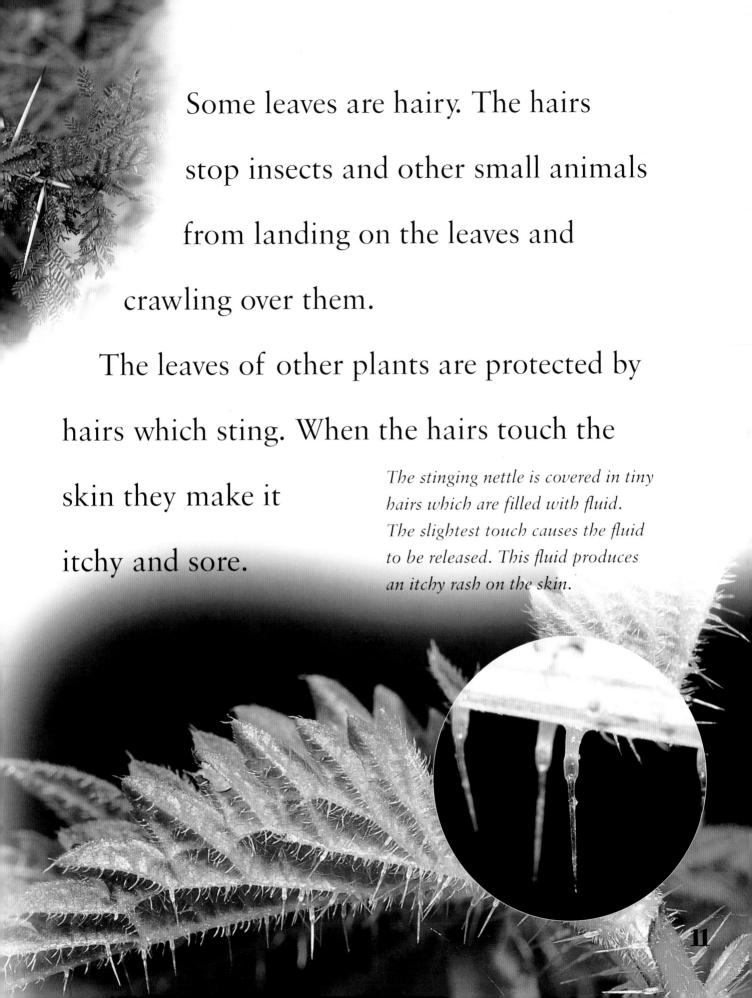

Some leaves are hairy. The hairs stop insects and other small animals from landing on the leaves and crawling over them.

The leaves of other plants are protected by hairs which sting. When the hairs touch the skin they make it itchy and sore.

The stinging nettle is covered in tiny hairs which are filled with fluid. The slightest touch causes the fluid to be released. This fluid produces an itchy rash on the skin.

Leaf fall

In autumn, the days are shorter and cooler. The leaves of some trees and **shrubs** start to change colour. They turn from green to shades of yellow, orange and red.

The leaves of deciduous trees start to change colour in September and October.

*In autumn, the ground below woodland trees in Europe and North America is covered with a thick mat of fallen leaves. These leaves rot and **break down** quickly and by summer they will have disappeared.*

Then the leaves drop off the plant. The plants are bare in winter and in spring they grow new leaves. Plants that lose their leaves in autumn are called **deciduous** plants.

Some of the best **autumn colours** are seen in parts of North America.

Many people travel to North America in the autumn to see the beautiful colours of the trees.

Special leaves

Most plants use their leaves to make food. A few plants use their leaves to catch their food! The pitcher plant has a leaf that is shaped like a jug. The jug has a lid and it is filled with fluid. Flies and other small insects crawl into the jug and then slip down the sides.

This pitcher plant grows in tropical rainforests. Many insects live on and near the forest floor so there is a lot of food about.

They drown in the fluid. The insect bodies are broken down and the plant takes in the **nutrients**.

The hairs on the leaf of the Venus flytrap are so sensitive that they can detect when a small insect lands on the surface of its leaves.

A plant called a Venus flytrap has leaves with sharp **spines**. As soon as an insect lands on one of these leaves, the leaf shuts, trapping the insect inside.

The sundew plant grows in wet, boggy places where the soil is poor. The plant gets its nutrients from the bodies of insects that become trapped in the sticky hairs on its leaves.

Supporting stems

The stem of a plant supports the leaves. It holds them out so that they can catch the sunlight. Stems vary in shape. Most plants have round stems, but some have stems that are square or **ridged**.

A tall plant needs a lot of support so it has a thicker stem.

The stem of this plant is square shaped.

The sunflower has a strong stem which is covered in small hairs.

Some plants have soft stems that die back at the end of the summer. Trees and shrubs produce woody stems that survive the winter. Each year their stems get longer and thicker.

*A horse chestnut twig. When leaves fall they leave a **scar** on the bark. The position of the scars shows how much the twig has grown in one year.*

The length of twig between these two scars is one year's growth.

Woody trunks

Trees are the tallest plants in the world. They need a thick woody trunk for support. Each year, the **trunk** gets larger as the tree produces new wood. The outside of the trunk is covered in bark.

The giant sequoias are trees found in North America. They can grow to heights of more than 100m and can live for thousands of years.

The baobab tree grows in dry places of Africa. It can store water in its thick trunk. It loses its leaves during the dry months of the year.

Trees are often **harvested** for their wood. The wood is mostly used in buildings and for making furniture. In many parts of the world, wood is used as a fuel for heating and cooking.

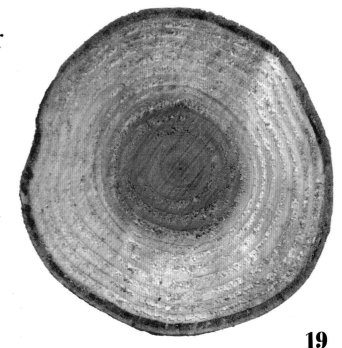

When you look at a tree trunk you can see **growth rings***. There is one ring for each year of the tree's life. You can work out the age of the tree by counting the number of growth rings.*

Taking hold

Climbing plants have many different ways of clambering over other plants to reach the light.

Gardeners place runner beans and peas at the base of a stick or cane. As the plant stem grows and gets longer, it wraps itself around the supports.

The pea plant produces tendrils which wrap themselves around other stems like a corkscrew.

The liana starts off life on the ground and slowly twines upwards around the trunk of a tree. Some liana stems are swollen with water which people can use as a source of water when they are in the rainforest.

Lianas are **twining plants** that are found in rainforests. The thick branches of a liana wrap themselves around the trunks of the largest trees.

Some climbing plants have **tendrils** which wrap themselves around other plants and fences. The tendrils hold the plant in position.

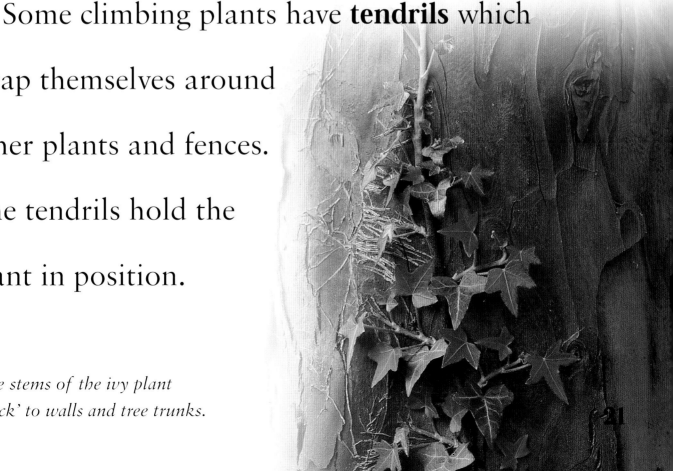

The stems of the ivy plant 'stick' to walls and tree trunks.

21

Roots

Roots spread through the soil and hold a plant firmly in the ground. They take up water and nutrients from the soil. The water and nutrients are carried through the roots to the shoot.

This tree is growing on rocky ground. Its roots are growing over the surface as they cannot grow down through the rocks.

Root hairs are tiny threads which grow from the main roots. These hairs allow the plant to take up much more water. The deepest roots go down many metres into the ground.

Cactus plants grow in hot, dry deserts. Some cacti have deep roots to reach underground water.

Root hairs grow just behind the tip of plant roots. They take up water and nutrients from the ground.

Some cactus plants have roots which spread out over a wide area so they can take in as much water as possible.

23

Types of roots

There are several different types of roots. Dandelions and thistles have a single thick root which grows down into the soil. This is called a **tap root**. Grasses have a network of fine, thin roots which spread out through the soil.

Tap root

Many weeds, such as this dandelion have a large tap root that extends deep into the ground making it difficult to pull up the plant.

Epiphytes are found growing on trees in the rainforest. They take up water from the moist air.

Some plants do not have roots which grow into the ground. In the rainforest there are plants which grow on  the branches of the trees. These plants are called **epiphytes** (epi-fites).

Pot plants usually have a root system that is made up of lots of smaller roots. This plant is ready to be repotted into a larger pot.

Underground storage

Many plants use their roots to store food.

The roots swell up during the summer months.

Vegetables such as carrots, beetroot and parsnips are the roots of plants. Much of our sugar comes from the swollen root of the sugar beet plant.

Carrots produce an orange root that swells up with food during the summer.

26

Sugar beet roots. These roots are taken to a factory where the sugar is removed.

A bulb is formed from the swollen bases of leaves. During the summer the plant moves food to the base of its leaves. The bulb survives the winter in the ground. In spring, new leaves appear above the ground. The plant uses the stored food in the bulb until its new leaves are large enough to start producing food.

In early spring, the bulb starts to grow and new leaves push up from the top.

Investigate!

Making new plants

It is easy to take cuttings from a geranium plant to produce new plants.

Carefully remove the leaves at the bottom of the geranium cutting and place it in a glass of water.

What to do:
- Remove a piece of shoot about 10 cm long. Remove the bottom pair of leaves.
- Stand the shoot in a small jar of water on a window ledge and leave it there until you see tiny roots growing from the bottom of the shoot.
- Plant the cutting in a small pot of compost.
- Water it well and place the pot in a plastic bag. Leave on a window ledge until you see new leaves appearing.

Within a month or so you should have a new plant.

How plants take up water

Always ask an adult for help when using sharp objects such as knives.

Celery has a white fleshy stem. You can see how water moves up a celery stem using coloured water.

What to do:

- Take a piece of celery stem and place the bottom in a small jar of coloured water.
- You can colour the water using ink or food colouring. Leave the celery in the water for a few hours so the water can move up the stem.
- Remove the celery from the water and place it on a chopping board.
- Using a knife, cut the celery into shorter pieces. Look at the cut ends. You should be able to see dots of colour. These mark the tubes through which the water moves up the plant.

The coloured water is drawn up into the celery.

Drying leaves

Dried leaves can be used to decorate greetings cards and other presents.

What to do:

A good time to collect your leaves is in autumn when they have changed colour.

- Collect leaves of different shapes and colours.
- Dry them by placing them between sheets of newspaper, weighted down by a pile of heavy books.

Collect leaves of different colours and shapes.

29

Glossary

autumn colours The yellow, orange and red colours of leaves during the autumn.

break down To rot and die.

bulb An underground store of food made from the swollen bases of leaves.

carbon dioxide A colourless gas in the air.

chlorophyll (klor-o-fill) The name of the green substance found in leaves and stems.

compound leaves Leaves that are made up of several leaflets.

deciduous A plant that drops its leaves in autumn or at the end of the growing season.

epiphytes Plants that grow on the branches of larger plants, but without harming them.

growth rings The new wood that is laid down in the trunk of a tree each year.

harvested Gathered or collected.

lianas Twining plants found growing up trees in rainforests.

mid rib The largest vein which runs up the centre of a leaf.

nutrients Substances that a plant needs for healthy growth.

oxygen A colourless gas found in the air and in water that animals and plants need to survive.

petiole The stalk of a leaf.

ridged Having raised sections, as on a stem.

scar A mark left on the bark of a twig made by a leaf dropping off.

shoot The part of the plant above the ground, with stems and leaves.

shrubs Small tree-like bushes or plants.

spiky Covered in sharp points.

spines Large thorns with sharp pointed ends.

tap root The main root of some plants that is swollen with food.

tendrils Curling shoots that a plant uses to hang on to a support, such as a stem.

trunk The main stem of a tree.

twining plants Plants that wrap themselves around other plants as they grow.

variegated A leaf that is partly green and partly white or yellow.

veins Structures running through a leaf that help to support it.

Index

32